D1712535

BIG
BEASTS

Polar Bear

Stephanie Turnbull

Published by Smart Apple Media
P.O. Box 1329
Mankato, MN 56002

Printed in the United States of America,
at Corporate Graphics in North Mankato, Minnesota.

Designed by Hel James
Edited by Mary-Jane Wilkins

Library of Congress Cataloging-in-Publication Data

Turnbull, Stephanie.
  Polar bear / Steph Turnbull.
     p. cm. -- (Big beasts)
  Includes index.
  Summary: "An introduction on polar bears, the big beasts in the
Arctic. Describes how polar bears move, find food, communicate,
and care for their young"--Provided by publisher.
  ISBN 978-1-59920-836-7 (hardcover, library bound)
  1. Polar bear--Juvenile literature. I. Title.
  QL737.C27T875 2013
  599.786--dc23
                         2012004115

Photo acknowledgements
l = left, r = right, t = top, b = bottom
page 1 Uryadnikov Sergey/Shutterstock; 3 iStockphoto/
Thinkstock; 5 Uryadnikov Sergey/Shutterstock; 6 iStockphoto/
Thinkstock; 7 BMCL/Shutterstock; 8 Ingram Publishing/
Thinkstock; 9 iStockphoto/Thinkstock; 10 VikOl/Shutterstock;
11 iStockphoto/Thinkstock; 12 Hemera/Thinkstock; 13 Jacqueline
Abromeit/Shutterstock; 14 Jacqueline Abromeit/Shutterstock;
15 Lilyana Vynogradova/Shutterstock; 16 Colette3/Shutterstock;
17 iStockphoto/Thinkstock; 18 Tom Brakefield/Thinkstock;
19 Uryadnikov Sergey/Shutterstock; 20-21 iStockphoto/
Thinkstock; 22t Catalin Petolea/Shutterstock; l xstockerx/
Shutterstock, b Wild Arctic Pictures/Shutterstock;
23 Tyler Olson/Shutterstock
Cover Sergey Smolin/Shutterstock

DAD0503
042012
9 8 7 6 5 4 3 2 1

Contents

Polar bears are

massive!

Arctic Giants

Polar bears are the **biggest** meat-eating land animals in the world.

They live on the icy lands and frozen sea of the Arctic.

Body fat and **thick** fur keep them warm.

4

On the Move

Hungry polar bears pad silently through the white wilderness.

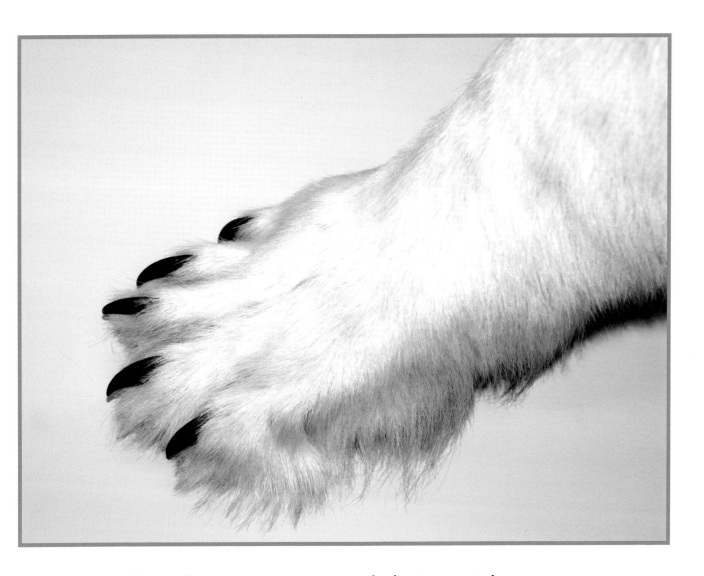

Four huge paws spread their weight
so they don't sink in snow.

Short, curved claws help them grip the ice.

Smelling Skills

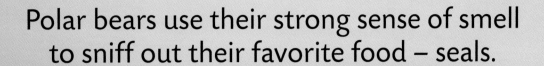

Polar bears use their strong sense of smell
to sniff out their favorite food – seals.

They can even smell seals hiding under snow.

Fat, juicy seals
give polar bears
lots of energy.

Attack!

Polar bears wait
patiently by water
for seals to pop up.

Often they find seal dens and **SMASH** the roof. Sometimes they creep close to seals, then sprint forward and **pounce!**

Killing Machines

Polar bears SWAT seals with their front paws, then BITE them with razor-sharp teeth.

Their long front teeth sink deep into prey.

If they can't find
seals, they eat fish
and other animals.

13

Super Swimmers

Polar bears love water.
They are fantastic swimmers.

They hold their
breath and dive
underwater to
catch prey.

They swim to keep clean
and cool, then roll on
snow to dry their fur.

Watch Out!

Polar bears get very angry if another bear tries to steal their food.

They grrrrowl, hissss, SNAP their teeth, and stand up tall on their back legs.

If one bear doesn't back off, they FIGHT!

Cute Cubs

In winter, female
bears dig a den
in the snow and
have babies.

Usually two cubs are born.

They stay in the cozy den until spring, drinking their mother's milk.

Then it's time to explore!

Growing Up

Cubs learn
to swim and
hunt for food.

Mother bears protect them
from hungry wolves and
fierce male polar bears.

BIG Facts

Polar bears can be longer than you and a friend lying end to end.

New cubs are the size of a guinea pig, but adult males weigh more than two tigers.

Polar bears may attack animals as big as reindeer, walruses, and whales.

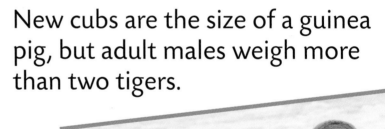

Polar bear paw prints
are bigger than a
page of this book.

Useful Words

Arctic
The cold area of land and sea around the North Pole.

cub
A baby polar bear. Cubs are deaf and blind when they are born.

den
A hidden hole or shelter.

prey
An animal that is hunted by another animal.

Index

Web Link
Go to this website to watch amazing videos of polar bears.
www.bbc.co.uk/nature/life/Polar_bear